INTERSTITIAL COOKBOOK FOR BEGINNERS

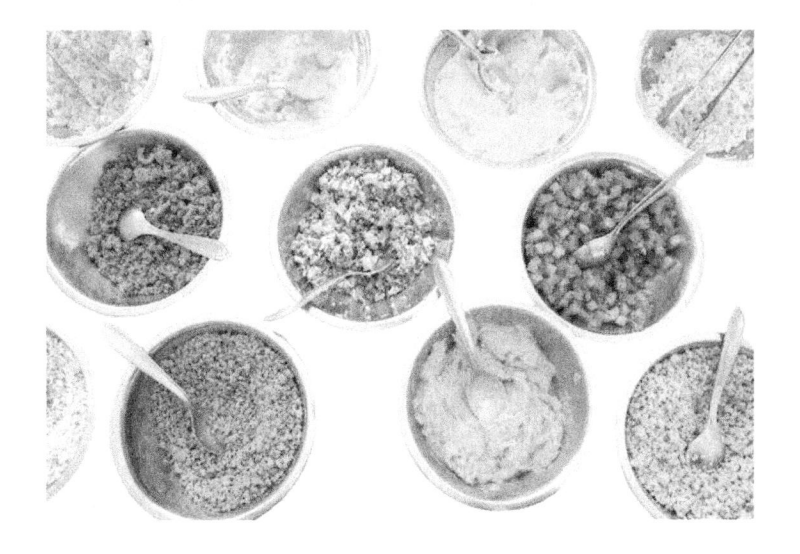

The Basics of an IC-Friendly Diet: What to Eat and What to Avoid

Linda Carlucci

Copyright © 2024 by Linda Carlucci

All rights reserved. No part of this book may be reproduced, stored, or transmitted by any means whether auditory, graphic, mechanical, or electronic without written permission of the author, except in the case of brief excerpts used in critical articles and reviews.

All the people depicted in stock imagery are models, and such images are being used for illustrative purposes only.

DISCLAIMER

This cookbook is intended to provide general information and recipes.

The recipes provided in this cookbook are not intended to replace or be a substitute for medical advice from a physician.

The reader should consult a healthcare professional for any specific medical advice, diagnosis or treatment.

Any specific dietary advice provided in this cookbook is not intended to replace or be a substitute for medical advice from a physician.

The author is not responsible or liable for any adverse effects experienced by readers of this cookbook as a result of following the recipes or dietary advice provided.

The author makes no representations or warranties of any kind (express or implied) as to the accuracy, completeness, reliability or suitability of the recipes provided in this cookbook.

The author disclaims any and all liability for any damages arising out of the use or misuse of the recipes provided in this cookbook. The reader must also take care to ensure that the recipes provided in this cookbook are prepared and cooked safely.

The recipes provided in this cookbook are for informational purposes only and should not be used as a substitute for professional medical advice, diagnosis or treatment.

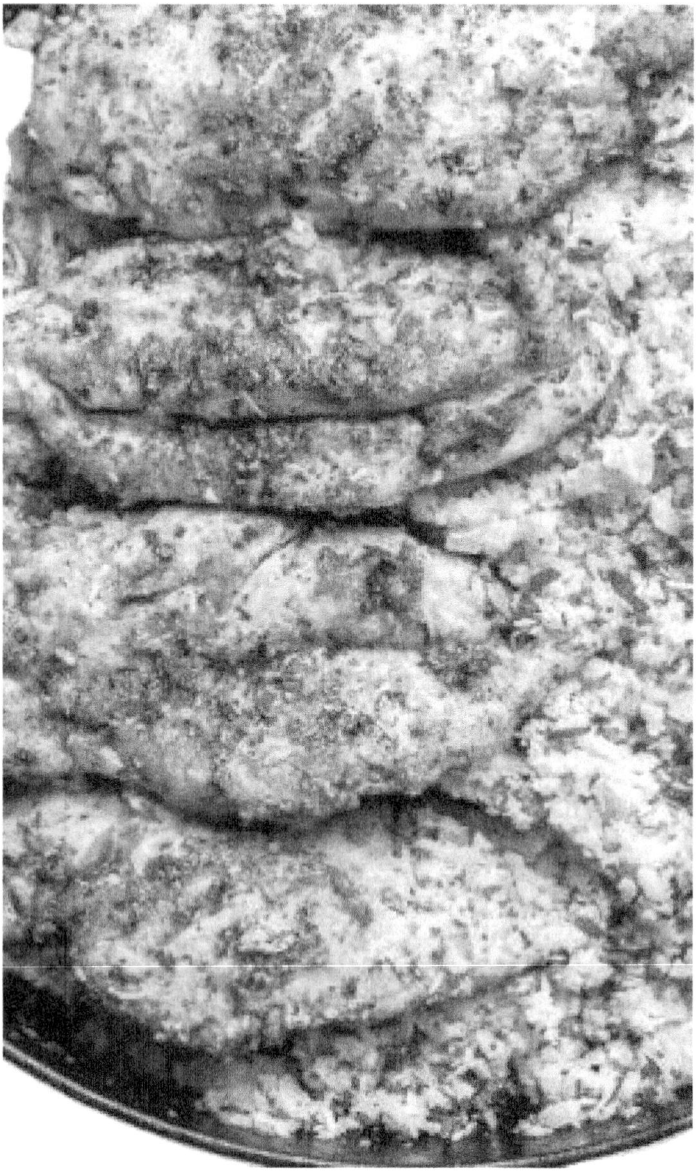

TABLE OF CONTENTS

INTRODUCTION 9

CHAPTER 1 11

COMMON SYMPTOMS OF INTERSTITIAL CYSTITIS 11

FOODS TO AVOID WHEN DEALING WITH INTERSTITIAL CYSTITIS 12

HEALTHY FOODS TO EAT FOR RELIEF 14

CHAPTER 2 17

14-DAY MEAL PLAN 17

CHAPTER 3 21

NUTRITIOUS RECIPES FOR AN INTERSTITIAL CYSTITIS DIET 21

BREAKFAST 21

Overnight Apple and Almond Oats 21

IC-Friendly Blueberry Smoothie 22

IC-Friendly Breakfast Frittata Cups 23

Quick Oats Granola 24

Blueberry Breakfast Casserole 26

Strawberry Muffins 27

Pear and Applesauce 28

Pumpkin Apple Streusel Muffins 29

Oatmeal Parfait 31

Cinnamon Pear Smoothie 32

LUNCH 33

Wheatena with Pecans 33

Omelet with Kale and Broccoli 34

Avocado Toast 35

Oatmeal with Almond and Banana 36

Roast Turkey Sandwich 37

Cobb Salad 38

Grilled Cheese Sandwich 39

Quinoa Burrito Bowl 40

Pasta with White Clam Sauce 41

Quinoa and Almond Bowl 42

DINNER 43

Grilled Tuna Salad with Broccoli 43

Hamburger 44
Broiled Veal Chop 45
Chicken and Apricot Rice 46
Broiled Shrimp and Couscous 47
Cheesy Zucchini Quiche 48
Crunchy Potato Casserole 50
Smoked Bacon Broccoli Cheddar Crustless Quiche 51
Smoked Bacon Basil Pesto and Chicken Pizza 52
Hummus Salad Dressing 53
DESSERT 54
Raspberry Peanut Butter Summer Cake 54
Banana Cookies 55
Cream Cheese Pie Cake 56
Blueberry Maple Pie 57
Banana and Apple Cake 58
SOUPS AND STEWS 59
Overnight Chicken Soup 59
Broccoli Cheddar Soup 60

Potato Mild Fresh Cheese Soup 62

Fennel Carrot Soup 63

Chicken Gnocchi Soup 64

POULTRY MAINS 65

Garlic Peanut Butter Chicken with Parmesan Basmati Rice 65

One-Pan Chicken with Gravy 67

Baked Chicken Drumsticks 68

Rosemary Turkey Bowl 69

One-Pan Turkey and Potatoes 70

SEAFOOD MAINS 71

Baked Salmon with Herbs 71

Grilled Shrimp Skewers 72

Poached Cod with Dill 73

Steamed Mussels in White Wine Sauce 74

Broiled Flounder with Peanut Butter 75

CONCLUSION 77

INTRODUCTION

Interstitial cystitis (IC), also known as painful bladder syndrome, is a chronic condition characterized by bladder pressure, bladder pain, and sometimes pelvic pain, ranging from mild discomfort to severe pain.

The cause of IC is not well understood, but it is believed to involve a defect in the bladder lining, allowing irritating substances in urine to penetrate the bladder, leading to inflammation and pain.

Diet plays a crucial role in managing IC symptoms, as certain foods and beverages can irritate the bladder and worsen symptoms.

In general, people with IC are advised to avoid or limit foods and beverages that can irritate the bladder, such as spicy foods, acidic foods and drinks (like tomatoes, citrus fruits, and coffee), artificial sweeteners, alcohol, and carbonated beverages.

Instead, they are encouraged to focus on a diet that is bland and low in potential bladder irritants. This may include foods like lean proteins, whole grains, non-citrus fruits, and vegetables that are not high in acidity.

Some people with IC find that following a low-oxalate diet helps manage their symptoms.

Oxalates are compounds found in many foods that can contribute to bladder irritation.

Foods high in oxalates include spinach, rhubarb, beets, some nuts, chocolate, and tea.

By reducing the intake of these foods, you may experience a reduction in bladder symptoms.

It's important for you with IC to pay attention to your body's responses to different foods and beverages, as triggers can vary from person to person.

Keeping a food diary can help identify potential triggers, making it easier to manage symptoms through dietary changes. In addition to dietary modifications, other treatments for IC may include medications, bladder instillations, physical therapy, and nerve stimulation.

CHAPTER 1

COMMON SYMPTOMS OF INTERSTITIAL CYSTITIS

1. **Painful urination:** Anyone with IC often experience pain, pressure, or discomfort in the bladder and pelvic area during urination.

2. **Frequent urination:** People with IC may need to urinate more often than usual, sometimes as frequently as every 10 to 15 minutes.

3. **Urgency:** There is a strong and sudden urge to urinate that is difficult to delay, often leading to frequent trips to the bathroom.

4. **Pelvic pain:** Chronic pelvic pain, often described as a dull ache or pressure in the lower abdomen, is a common symptom of IC.

5. **Pain during intercourse:** Some individuals with IC experience pain or discomfort during sexual intercourse, known as dyspareunia.

6. **Nighttime urination:** Many people with IC wake up multiple times during the night to urinate, disrupting their sleep.

7. **Incomplete emptying of the bladder:** Despite frequent urination, individuals with IC may feel like their bladder is not completely empty.
8. **Other urinary symptoms:** Some people with IC may experience blood in the urine (hematuria) or cloudy urine.

FOODS TO AVOID WHEN DEALING WITH INTERSTITIAL CYSTITIS

When dealing with interstitial cystitis (IC), it's often recommended to avoid or limit foods and beverages that can irritate the bladder and worsen symptoms. Some common trigger foods and beverages to avoid include:

1. **Acidic foods:** Citrus fruits and juices, tomatoes, and products containing these ingredients can irritate the bladder.
2. **Spicy foods:** Spices like chili powder, curry, and hot peppers can irritate the bladder and worsen symptoms.
3. **Caffeinated beverages:** Coffee, tea, and some sodas contain caffeine, which can irritate the bladder and increase urinary urgency.

4. **Alcoholic beverages:** Alcohol can irritate the bladder and worsen symptoms.
5. **Carbonated beverages:** The carbonation in sodas and sparkling water can irritate the bladder.
6. **Artificial sweeteners:** Some artificial sweeteners, such as aspartame and saccharin, can irritate the bladder.
7. **High-oxalate foods:** Foods high in oxalates, such as spinach, rhubarb, beets, nuts, and chocolate, can irritate the bladder.
8. **Processed foods:** Processed foods often contain additives and preservatives that can irritate the bladder.
9. **Highly spiced foods:** Foods with strong spices and seasonings, such as hot sauce, curry powder, and vinegar-based dressings, can irritate the bladder.
10. **Highly acidic foods:** Foods like vinegar, pineapple, and cranberries can irritate the bladder.

HEALTHY FOODS TO EAT FOR RELIEF

1. **Water:** Staying hydrated is important for overall bladder health. Drinking plenty of water can help flush out irritants and dilute urine, reducing bladder irritation.
2. **Low-acid fruits:** Non-citrus fruits such as bananas, pears, and apples are less likely to irritate the bladder compared to citrus fruits.
3. **Vegetables:** Most vegetables are well-tolerated by people with IC. Go for non-acidic choices like broccoli, carrots, green beans, and zucchini.
4. **Lean proteins:** Choose lean sources of protein such as chicken, turkey, and fish. Avoid processed meats and high-fat cuts of meat.
5. **Whole grains:** Foods like oats, brown rice, and whole-grain bread are good sources of fiber and can be part of a bladder-friendly diet.
6. **Dairy alternatives:** Some people with IC find relief by avoiding dairy products and opting for dairy alternatives like almond milk or coconut milk.

7. **Herbal teas:** Chamomile tea and other herbal teas that are non-caffeinated can be soothing and hydrating.
8. **Cooking oils:** Use olive oil or canola oil instead of butter or margarine, which may be irritating to the bladder.
9. **Low-oxalate foods:** If you find that oxalates trigger your symptoms, focus on low-oxalate foods such as cauliflower, cucumbers, and grapes.
10. **Probiotic-rich foods:** Some studies suggest that probiotics may help improve symptoms of IC. Foods like yogurt, kefir, and sauerkraut are good sources of probiotics.

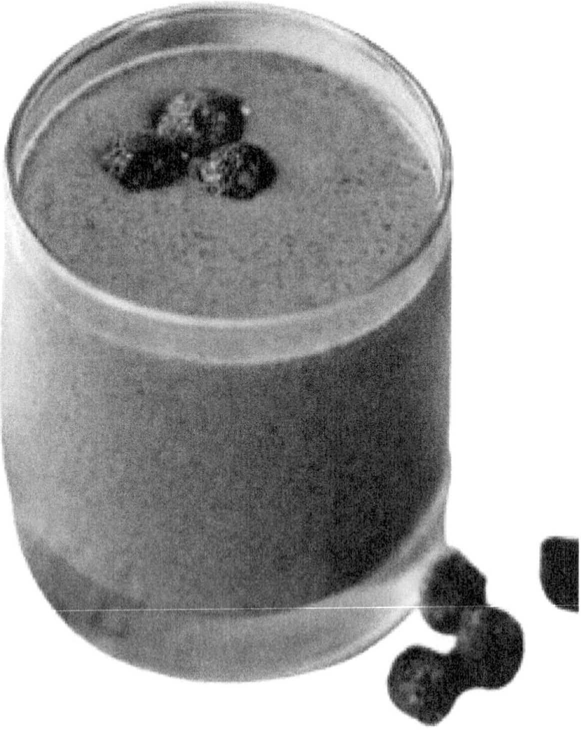

CHAPTER 2

14-DAY MEAL PLAN

DAY 1

Breakfast: Overnight Apple and Almond Oats

Lunch: Wheatena with Pecans

Dinner: Grilled Tuna Salad with Broccoli

DAY 2

Breakfast: IC-Friendly Blueberry Smoothie

Lunch: Omelet with Kale and Broccoli

Dinner: Hamburger

DAY 3

Breakfast: IC-Friendly Breakfast Frittata Cups

Lunch: Avocado Toast

Dinner: Broiled Veal Chop

DAY 4

Breakfast: Quick Oats Granola

Lunch: Oatmeal with Banana

Dinner: Chicken and Apricot Rice

DAY 5

Breakfast: Blueberry Breakfast Casserole

Lunch: Roast Turkey Sandwich

Dinner: Broiled Shrimp and Couscous

DAY 6

Breakfast: Strawberry Muffins

Lunch: Cobb Salad

Dinner: Cheesy Zucchini Quiche

DAY 7

Breakfast: Pear and Applesauce

Lunch: Grilled mild fresh Cheese Sandwich

Dinner: Crunchy Potato Casserole

DAY 8

Breakfast: Pumpkin Apple Streusel Muffins

Lunch: Quinoa Burrito Bowl

Dinner: Smoked Bacon Broccoli Cheddar Crustless Quiche

DAY 9

Breakfast: Oatmeal Parfait

Lunch: Pasta with White Clam Sauce

Dinner: Smoked Bacon Basil Pesto and Chicken Pizza

DAY 10

Breakfast: Cinnamon Pear Smoothie

Lunch: Quinoa and Almond Bowl

Dinner: Hummus Salad Dressing

DAY 11

Breakfast: Overnight Apple and Almond Oats

Lunch: Wheatena with Pecans

Dinner: Grilled Tuna Salad with Broccoli

DAY 12

Breakfast: IC-Friendly Blueberry Smoothie

Lunch: Omelet with Kale and Broccoli

Dinner: Hamburger

DAY 13

Breakfast: IC-Friendly Breakfast Frittata Cups

Lunch: Avocado Toast

Dinner: Broiled Veal Chop

DAY 14

Breakfast: Quick Oats Granola

Lunch: Oatmeal with Banana

Dinner: Chicken and Apricot Rice

CHAPTER 3

NUTRITIOUS RECIPES FOR AN INTERSTITIAL CYSTITIS DIET

BREAKFAST

Overnight Apple and Almond Oats

Preparation Time: 10 minutes + overnight soaking

Serves: 2

Calories: 100 **Protein:** 8g **Sodium:** 30mg

Ingredients:

1 cup old-fashioned oats

1 cup unsweetened almond milk

1/2 cup grated apple

2 tablespoons almond butter

1 tablespoon stevia or maple syrup (optional, replace with stevia for IC diet)

1/2 teaspoon cinnamon

1/4 cup sliced almonds (optional, omit for IC diet)

Method of Preparation:

1. In a bowl, combine oats, almond milk, grated apple, almond butter, sweetener (if using), and cinnamon.
2. Stir well, cover, and refrigerate overnight.
3. In the morning, stir the oats and top with sliced almonds if desired. Serve cold.

IC-Friendly Blueberry Smoothie

Preparation Time: 5 minutes

Serves: 2

Calories: 150 **Protein:** 3g **Sodium:** 20mg

Ingredients:

1 cup unsweetened almond milk

1/2 cup frozen blueberries

1/2 banana

1 tablespoon chia seeds

1 tablespoon almond butter

1/2 teaspoon vanilla extract

Ice cubes (optional)

Method of Preparation:

1. In a blender, combine almond milk, blueberries, banana, chia seeds, almond butter, and vanilla extract.
2. Blend until smooth.
3. Add ice cubes if desired and blend again until smooth. Serve immediately.

IC-Friendly Breakfast Frittata Cups

Preparation Time: 25 minutes

Serves: 4

Calories: 200 **Protein:** 10g **Sodium:** 150mg

Ingredients:

6 large eggs

1/4 cup unsweetened almond milk

1/2 cup diced zucchini

1/2 cup diced carrots

1/4 cup chopped cooked chicken (optional, omit for vegetarian)

1/4 teaspoon dried thyme

Method of Preparation:

1. Preheat the oven to 350°F (175°C) and grease a muffin tin.
2. In a bowl, whisk together eggs, almond milk, and thyme,
3. Stir in zucchini, carrots, and chicken (if using).
4. Pour the egg mixture into the prepared muffin tin, filling each cup about 2/3 full.
5. Bake for 20-25 minutes, or until the frittata cups are set and lightly golden.
6. Allow to cool slightly before serving.

Quick Oats Granola

Preparation Time: 20 minutes

Serves: 4

Calories: 180 **Protein:** 4g **Sodium:** 20mg

Ingredients:

1 cup quick oats

1/4 cup chopped almonds

1/4 cup unsweetened shredded coconut

2 tablespoons stevia

1 tablespoon coconut oil

1/2 teaspoon cinnamon

Method of Preparation:

1. Preheat the oven to 300°F (150°C) and line a baking sheet with parchment paper.
2. In a bowl, combine oats, almonds, coconut, stevia, coconut oil, and cinnamon.
3. Spread the mixture evenly on the prepared baking sheet.
4. Bake for 15-20 minutes, stirring halfway through, until golden brown.
5. Allow the granola to cool completely before serving.

Blueberry Breakfast Casserole

Preparation Time: 45 minutes

Serves: 6

Calories: 220 **Protein:** 8g **Sodium:** 150mg

Ingredients:

6 slices whole wheat bread, cubed

1 cup unsweetened almond milk

2 eggs

1 teaspoon vanilla extract

1/2 teaspoon cinnamon

2 cups fresh or frozen blueberries

2 tablespoons stevia

Method of Preparation:

1. Preheat the oven to 350°F (175°C) and grease a baking dish.
2. In a large bowl, whisk together almond milk, eggs, vanilla extract, cinnamon, and stevia.

3. Add the bread cubes and blueberries to the bowl and toss to coat.
4. Pour the mixture into the prepared baking dish.
5. Bake for 30-35 minutes, or until the casserole is set and lightly browned.
6. Allow to cool slightly before serving.

Strawberry Muffins

Preparation Time: 30 minutes

Serves: 6

Calories: 180

Protein: 5g

Sodium: 100mg

Ingredients:

1 cup oat flour (blend oats in a blender until fine)

1/2 teaspoon baking soda

1/4 teaspoon salt

1/4 cup unsweetened applesauce

1/4 cup stevia

1 egg

1 teaspoon vanilla extract

1/2 cup diced strawberries

Method of Preparation:

1. Preheat the oven to 350°F (175°C) and grease a muffin tin or line with muffin liners.
2. In a large bowl, whisk together oat flour, baking soda, and salt.
3. In a separate bowl, mix together applesauce, stevia, egg, and vanilla extract.
4. Add the wet ingredients to the dry ingredients and mix until just combined.
5. Gently fold in the diced strawberries.
6. Divide the batter evenly among the muffin cups.
7. Bake for 15-18 minutes, or until a toothpick inserted into the center comes out clean.
8. Allow to cool slightly before serving.

Pear and Applesauce

Preparation Time: 10 minutes

Serves: 2

Calories: 120 **Protein:** 1g **Sodium:** 5mg

Ingredients:

1 ripe pear, peeled and chopped

1/2 cup unsweetened applesauce

1/2 teaspoon cinnamon

Method of Preparation:

1. In a blender, combine pear, applesauce, and cinnamon.
2. Blend until smooth.
3. Serve chilled.

Pumpkin Apple Streusel Muffins

Preparation Time: 30 minutes

Serves: 6

Calories: 200 **Protein:** 3g **Sodium:** 100mg

Ingredients:

1 cup oat flour

1/2 cup canned pumpkin puree

1/2 cup unsweetened applesauce

1/4 cup stevia or maple syrup (optional, replace with stevia for IC diet)

1 teaspoon baking powder

1/2 teaspoon baking soda

1/2 teaspoon cinnamon

1/4 teaspoon nutmeg

1/4 teaspoon salt

Streusel topping (optional):

2 tablespoons oat flour

2 tablespoons chopped pecans

1 tablespoon coconut sugar

1/2 teaspoon cinnamon

1 tablespoon melted coconut oil

Method of Preparation:

1. Preheat the oven to 350°F (175°C) and grease a muffin tin or line with muffin liners.

2. In a large bowl, whisk together oat flour, baking powder, baking soda, cinnamon, nutmeg, and salt.
3. In a separate bowl, mix together pumpkin puree, applesauce, stevia.
4. Add the wet ingredients to the dry ingredients and mix until just combined.
5. Divide the batter evenly among the muffin cups.
6. If using streusel topping, mix all streusel ingredients in a small bowl and sprinkle over the muffins.
7. Bake for 18-20 minutes, or until a toothpick inserted into the center comes out clean.
8. Allow to cool slightly before serving.

Oatmeal Parfait

Preparation Time: 10 minutes

Serves: 2

Calories: 180 **Protein:** 6g **Sodium:** 50mg

Ingredients:

1/2 cup rolled oats

1 cup unsweetened almond milk

1/2 teaspoon cinnamon

Almond

1/4 cup fresh berries

Method of Preparation:

1. In a bowl, combine rolled oats and almond milk.
2. Cover and refrigerate overnight.
3. In the morning, layer the oatmeal with cinnamon, almond and fresh berries in a serving glass or bowl.
4. Serve chilled.

Cinnamon Pear Smoothie

Preparation Time: 5 minutes

Serves: 2

Calories: 150 **Protein:** 2g **Sodium:** 10mg

Ingredients:

1 ripe pear, peeled and chopped

1/2 cup unsweetened almond milk

1/2 cup plain Greek yogurt

1/2 teaspoon cinnamon

Ice cubes (optional)

Method of Preparation:

1. In a blender, combine pear, almond milk, Greek yogurt, and cinnamon.
2. Add ice cubes if desired and blend until smooth.
3. Serve immediately.

LUNCH

Wheatena with Pecans

Preparation Time: 10 minutes

Serves: 2

Calories: 250 **Protein:** 6g **Sodium:** 10mg

Ingredients:

1/2 cup Wheatena cereal

1 1/2 cups water

1/4 cup chopped pecans

1 tablespoon stevia

Method of Preparation:

1. In a saucepan, bring water to a boil.
2. Stir in Wheatena cereal and reduce heat to low.
3. Simmer for 5 minutes, stirring occasionally.
4. Remove from heat and let stand for 2 minutes.
5. Serve hot, topped with chopped pecans and stevia.

Omelet with Kale and Broccoli

Preparation Time: 15 minutes

Serves: 2

Calories: 200 **Protein:** 12g **Sodium:** 150mg

Ingredients:

4 large eggs

1/4 cup unsweetened almond milk

1/2 cup chopped kale

1/2 cup chopped broccoli

Herbs

Method of Preparation:

1. In a bowl, whisk together eggs and almond milk.
2. Season with herbs.
3. Heat a non-stick skillet over medium heat and add the eggs.
4. Cook for 2-3 minutes, or until the eggs start to set.
5. Add kale and broccoli to one side of the omelet.
6. Fold the other side of the omelet over the vegetables.
7. Cook for another 2-3 minutes, or until the vegetables are tender and the eggs are cooked through.
8. Serve hot.

Avocado Toast

Preparation Time: 10 minutes

Serves: 2

Calories: 220 **Protein:** 5g **Sodium:** 50mg

Ingredients:

2 slices whole grain bread, toasted

1 ripe avocado, mashed

Herbs

Method of Preparation:

1. Spread mashed avocado evenly onto the toasted bread slices.
2. Season with herbs.
3. Serve immediately.

Oatmeal with Almond and Banana

Preparation Time: 10 minutes

Serves: 2

Calories: 300 **Protein:** 7g **Sodium:** 5mg

Ingredients:

1 cup rolled oats

2 cups water

1/4 cup chopped almond

1 banana, sliced

1 tablespoon stevia

Method of Preparation:

1. In a saucepan, bring water to a boil.

2. Stir in rolled oats and reduce heat to low.
3. Simmer for 5 minutes, stirring occasionally.
4. Remove from heat and let stand for 2 minutes.
5. Serve hot, topped with sliced banana, and stevia.

Roast Turkey Sandwich

Preparation Time: 15 minutes

Serves: 2

Calories: 250 **Protein:** 15g **Sodium:** 200mg

Ingredients:

4 slices whole grain bread, toasted

1/2-pound roasted turkey breast, sliced

1/2 avocado, sliced

Method of Preparation:

1. Layer turkey breast, avocado slices on two slices of bread.
2. Top with the remaining slices of bread to make two sandwiches.
3. Serve immediately.

Cobb Salad

Preparation Time: 20 minutes

Serves: 2

Calories: 300 **Protein:** 12g **Sodium:** 200mg

Ingredients:

4 cups mixed salad greens

1/2 cup diced turkey breast

1/2 avocado, diced

1/4 cup crumbled blue cheese

2 hard-boiled eggs, sliced

1/4 cup diced cucumber

1/4 cup diced red onion

2 tablespoons balsamic vinaigrette dressing

Method of Preparation:

1. In a large bowl, combine salad greens, turkey breast, avocado, blue cheese, hard-boiled eggs, cucumber, and red onion.

2. Drizzle with balsamic vinaigrette dressing and toss to coat.
3. Divide the salad between two plates and serve immediately.

Grilled Cheese Sandwich

Preparation Time: 10 minutes

Serves: 2

Calories: 300 **Protein:** 10g **Sodium:** 400mg

Ingredients:

4 slices whole grain bread

1/2 cup shredded cheddar cheese

1/2 cup shredded mozzarella cheese

1 tablespoon butter or olive oil (for cooking)

Method of Preparation:

1. Heat a non-stick skillet over medium heat.
2. Place two slices of bread on a work surface and sprinkle half of the cheddar cheese and half of the mozzarella cheese on each slice.

3. Top with the remaining slices of bread to make two sandwiches.
4. Spread butter or olive oil on the outside of each sandwich.
5. Place the sandwiches in the skillet and cook for 3-4 minutes per side, or until the bread is golden brown and the cheese is melted.
6. Serve hot.

Quinoa Burrito Bowl

Preparation Time: 20 minutes

Serves: 2

Calories: 350 **Protein:** 12g **Sodium:** 300mg

Ingredients:

1 cup cooked quinoa

1/2 cup black beans, drained and rinsed

1/2 cup corn kernels

1/2 avocado, sliced

1/4 cup chopped cilantro

Method of Preparation:

1. In a bowl, combine cooked quinoa, black beans, corn kernels, and cilantro.
2. Divide the quinoa mixture between two bowls.
3. Top with sliced avocado and salsa (if using).
4. Serve immediately.

Pasta with White Clam Sauce

Preparation Time: 20 minutes

Serves: 2

Calories: 400 **Protein:** 15g **Sodium:** 400mg

Ingredients:

6 ounces gluten-free pasta

1 tablespoon olive oil

2 cloves garlic, minced

Clam sauce

1/2 cup chopped canned clams, drained

1/4 cup chopped parsley

Method of Preparation:

1. Cook pasta according to package instructions.
2. Drain and set aside.
3. In a large skillet, heat olive oil over medium heat.
4. Add garlic with clam sauce and cook until fragrant, about 1 minute.
5. Bring to a simmer.
6. Stir in chopped clams and parsley.
7. Cook for 2-3 minutes.
8. Add cooked pasta to the skillet and toss to coat.
9. Season with herbs.
10. Serve hot.

Quinoa and Almond Bowl

Serves: 2

Preparation Time: 15 minutes

Calories: 300 **Protein:** 10g **Sodium:** 100mg

Ingredients:

1 cup cooked quinoa

1/4 cup sliced almonds

1/2 teaspoon cinnamon

1/2 cup unsweetened almond milk

Method of Preparation:

1. In a bowl, combine cooked quinoa, sliced almonds, and cinnamon.
2. Divide the quinoa mixture between two bowls.
3. Pour almond milk over the quinoa mixture.
4. Serve immediately.

DINNER

Grilled Tuna Salad with Broccoli

Preparation Time: 20 minutes

Serves: 2

Calories: 300 **Protein:** 25g **Sodium:** 200mg

Ingredients:

2 tuna steaks

2 cups broccoli florets

1 tablespoon olive oil

Herbs

Method of Preparation:

1. Preheat a grill or grill pan over medium-high heat.
2. Season tuna steaks with herbs.
3. Grill tuna steaks for 3-4 minutes per side, or until cooked to your liking.
4. In a separate pot, steam broccoli florets until tender.
5. Divide the broccoli and tuna between two plates.
6. Drizzle with olive oil.
7. Serve hot.

Hamburger

Preparation Time: 20 minutes

Serves: 2

Calories: 350 **Protein:** 20g **Sodium:** 300mg

Ingredients:

1/2-pound lean ground beef

2 whole grain hamburger buns

Lettuce leaves and onion slices for topping

Method of Preparation:

1. Divide the ground beef into two equal portions and shape into patties.
2. Season the patties with herbs.
3. Heat a grill or grill pan over medium-high heat.
4. Grill the patties for 4-5 minutes per side, or until cooked to your liking.
5. Toast the hamburger buns on the grill for 1-2 minutes.
6. Place the cooked patties on the bottom halves of the buns.
7. Top with lettuce and onion slices.
8. Serve hot.

Broiled Veal Chop

Preparation Time: 25 minutes

Serves: 2

Calories: 400 **Protein:** 30g **Sodium:** 200mg

Ingredients:

2 veal chops

1 tablespoon olive oil

1 teaspoon dried thyme

Method of Preparation:

1. Preheat the broiler.
2. Rub veal chops with olive oil and season with thyme.
3. Place veal chops on a broiler pan and broil for 5-6 minutes per side, or until cooked to your liking.
4. Serve hot.

Chicken and Apricot Rice

Preparation Time: 30 minutes

Serves: 2

Calories: 350 **Protein:** 20g **Sodium:** 300mg

Ingredients:

1 tablespoon olive oil

2 boneless, skinless chicken breasts, diced

1/2 onion, chopped

1/2 cup dried apricots, chopped

1 cup white rice

2 cups chicken broth

Herbs

Method of Preparation:
1. In a large skillet, heat olive oil over medium heat.
2. Add diced chicken breasts and onion to the skillet.
3. Cook until chicken is browned and onion is softened.
4. Stir in dried apricots, white rice, and chicken broth.
5. Bring to a boil, then reduce heat to low, cover, and simmer for 15-20 minutes, or until rice is tender and liquid is absorbed.
6. Season with herbs.
7. Serve hot.

Broiled Shrimp and Couscous

Preparation Time: 20 minutes

Serves: 2

Calories: 300 **Protein:** 25g **Sodium:** 400mg

Ingredients:

1/2-pound shrimp, peeled and deveined

1 tablespoon olive oil

1 teaspoon paprika

1 cup couscous

1 1/4 cups water

Method of Preparation:

1. Preheat the broiler.
2. In a bowl, toss shrimp with olive oil, and paprika.
3. Place shrimp on a broiler pan and broil for 2-3 minutes per side, or until shrimp are pink and opaque.
4. Meanwhile, prepare couscous according to package instructions.
5. Serve shrimp over couscous.

Cheesy Zucchini Quiche

Preparation Time: 45 minutes

Serves: 2

Calories: 400 Protein: 15g **Sodium:** 300mg

Ingredients:

1 refrigerated pie crust

1 cup shredded zucchini

1/2 cup shredded cheddar cheese

2 eggs

1/2 cup milk

Method of Preparation:

1. Preheat the oven to 375°F (190°C).
2. Press the pie crust into a 9-inch pie dish.
3. Sprinkle shredded zucchini and cheddar cheese over the pie crust.
4. In a bowl, whisk together eggs, and milk.
5. Pour egg mixture over the zucchini and cheese.
6. Bake for 30-35 minutes, or until the quiche is set and golden brown.
7. Allow to cool slightly before serving.

Crunchy Potato Casserole

Preparation Time: 1 hour

Serves: 2

Calories: 400 **Protein:** 10g **Sodium:** 300mg

Ingredients:

2 large potatoes, thinly sliced

1/2 cup shredded cheddar cheese

1/4 cup breadcrumbs

1/4 cup grated Parmesan cheese

2 tablespoons butter, melted

Method of Preparation:

1. Preheat the oven to 350°F (175°C).
2. In a bowl, combine sliced potatoes, cheddar cheese, breadcrumbs, Parmesan cheese, and butter.
3. Transfer the mixture to a greased baking dish.
4. Bake for 45-50 minutes, or until the potatoes are tender and the top is golden brown.
5. Serve hot.

Smoked Bacon Broccoli Cheddar Crustless Quiche

Preparation Time: 45 minutes

Serves: 2

Calories: 350 **Protein:** 15g **Sodium:** 400mg

Ingredients:

4 slices bacon, chopped

1 cup chopped broccoli

1/2 cup shredded cheddar cheese

4 eggs

1/2 cup milk

Method of Preparation:

1. Preheat the oven to 350°F (175°C).
2. In a skillet, cook bacon over medium heat until crispy.
3. Remove from skillet and drain on paper towels.
4. In the same skillet, add chopped broccoli and sauté until tender.

5. In a bowl, whisk together eggs, and milk.
6. Stir in cooked bacon, broccoli, and cheddar cheese.
7. Pour the mixture into a greased pie dish.
8. Bake for 30-35 minutes, or until the quiche is set and golden brown.
9. Allow to cool slightly before serving.

Smoked Bacon Basil Pesto and Chicken Pizza

Preparation Time: 30 minutes

Serves: 2

Calories: 400 **Protein:** 20g **Sodium:** 450mg

Ingredients:

1 pre-made pizza crust

1/4 cup basil pesto

1 cup cooked chicken breast, shredded

4 slices smoked bacon, cooked and chopped

1/2 cup shredded mozzarella cheese

1/4 cup grated Parmesan cheese

Method of Preparation:

1. Preheat the oven to 425°F (220°C).
2. Spread basil pesto evenly over the pizza crust.
3. Top with shredded chicken, chopped bacon, mozzarella cheese, and Parmesan cheese.
4. Bake for 12-15 minutes, or until the crust is golden brown and the cheese is melted and bubbly.
5. Allow to cool slightly before slicing and serving.

Hummus Salad Dressing

Preparation Time: 5 minutes

Serves: 2

Calories: 100 **Protein:** 3g **Sodium:** 150mg

Ingredients:

1/4 cup hummus

1 tablespoon olive oil

1/2 teaspoon dried oregano

Method of Preparation:

1. In a bowl, whisk together olive oil, and dried oregano.
2. Add the hummus to the mixture.
3. Serve over your favorite salad greens.

DESSERT

Raspberry Peanut Butter Summer Cake

Preparation Time: 45 minutes

Serves: 2

Calories: 300 **Protein:** 5g **Sodium:** 150mg

Ingredients:

1/2 cup raspberries

1/4 cup peanut butter

1/4 cup stevia

1/4 cup almond flour

1/4 teaspoon baking powder

1/4 teaspoon vanilla extract

Method of Preparation:

1. Preheat the oven to 350°F (175°C).
2. In a bowl, mash raspberries with a fork.
3. Stir in peanut butter, stevia, almond flour, baking powder, and vanilla extract until well combined.
4. Pour the batter into a greased baking dish.
5. Bake for 20-25 minutes, or until the cake is set and golden brown.
6. Allow to cool before serving.

Banana Cookies

Preparation Time: 25 minutes

Serves: 2

Calories: 250 **Protein:** 3g **Sodium:** 100mg

Ingredients:

1 ripe banana, mashed

1/2 cup oats

1/4 teaspoon cinnamon

Method of Preparation:

1. Preheat the oven to 350°F (175°C).
2. In a bowl, combine mashed banana, oats, chopped and cinnamon.
3. Drop spoonful of the mixture onto a baking sheet lined with parchment paper.
4. Bake for 15-20 minutes, or until the cookies are golden brown.
5. Allow to cool before serving.

Cream Cheese Pie Cake

Preparation Time: 1 hour

Serves: 2

Calories: 350 **Protein:** 5g **Sodium:** 200mg

Ingredients:

1/2 cup cream cheese, softened

1/4 cup sugar

1/4 cup sour cream

1/2 teaspoon vanilla extract

1 pre-made graham cracker crust

Method of Preparation:

1. In a bowl, beat cream cheese, sugar, sour cream, and vanilla extract until smooth.
2. Pour the mixture into the graham cracker crust.
3. Bake for 30-35 minutes, or until the filling is set.
4. Allow to cool before serving.

Blueberry Maple Pie

Preparation Time: 1 hour

Serves: 2

Calories: 300 **Protein:** 3g **Sodium:** 150mg

Ingredients:

1 cup blueberries

2 tablespoons maple syrup

1 tablespoon cornstarch

1 pre-made pie crust

Method of Preparation:

1. Preheat the oven to 350°F (175°C).
2. In a bowl, combine blueberries, maple syrup, and cornstarch.
3. Pour the blueberry mixture into the pie crust.
4. Bake for 30-35 minutes, or until the filling is bubbly and the crust is golden brown.
5. Allow to cool before serving.

Banana and Apple Cake

Preparation Time: 45 minutes

Serves: 2

Calories: 300 **Protein:** 4g **Sodium:** 150mg

Ingredients:

1 ripe banana, mashed

1 apple, peeled and grated

1/4 cup sugar

1/4 cup vegetable oil

1/2 teaspoon vanilla extract

1/2 cup flour

1/2 teaspoon baking soda

1/2 teaspoon cinnamon

Method of Preparation:

1. Preheat the oven to 350°F (175°C).
2. In a bowl, combine mashed banana, grated apple, sugar, vegetable oil, and vanilla extract.
3. Stir in flour, baking soda, and cinnamon until well combined.
4. Pour the batter into a greased baking dish.
5. Bake for 25-30 minutes, or until the cake is set and golden brown.
6. Allow to cool before serving.

SOUPS AND STEWS

Overnight Chicken Soup

Preparation Time: 8 hours (overnight)

Serves: 2

Calories: 250 **Protein:** 15g **Sodium:** 400mg

Ingredients:

1 pound chicken breast, cubed

4 cups chicken broth

1 onion, chopped

2 carrots, sliced

2 celery stalks, sliced

2 garlic cloves, minced

1 teaspoon dried thyme

Method of Preparation:

1. In a slow cooker, combine chicken breast, chicken broth, onion, carrots, celery, garlic, and thyme.
2. Cover and cook on low for 8 hours.
3. Serve hot.

Broccoli Cheddar Soup

Preparation Time: 30 minutes

Serves: 2

Calories: 300 **Protein:** 10g **Sodium:** 500mg

Ingredients:

2 tablespoons butter

1/2 onion, chopped

2 cups chopped broccoli florets

2 cups chicken or vegetable broth

1 cup milk

1 cup shredded cheddar cheese

Method of Preparation:

1. In a large pot, melt butter over medium heat.
2. Add onion and cook until softened.
3. Stir in broccoli florets and cook for 5 minutes.
4. Add chicken or vegetable broth and bring to a boil.
5. Reduce heat and simmer for 15-20 minutes, or until broccoli is tender.
6. Stir in milk and cheddar cheese until cheese is melted and soup is heated through.
7. Serve hot.

Potato Mild Fresh Cheese Soup

Preparation Time: 40 minutes

Serves: 2

Calories: 350 **Protein:** 10g **Sodium:** 40mg

Ingredients:

2 tablespoons butter

1/2 onion, chopped

2 potatoes, peeled and diced

2 cups chicken or vegetable broth

1 cup milk

1 cup shredded cheese

Method of Preparation:

1. In a large pot, melt butter over medium heat.
2. Add onion and cook until softened.
3. Stir in diced potatoes and cook for 5 minutes.
4. Add chicken or vegetable broth and bring to a boil.
5. Reduce heat and simmer for 15-20 minutes, or until potatoes are tender.

6. Stir in milk and cheddar cheese until cheese is melted and soup is heated through.
7. Serve hot.

Fennel Carrot Soup

Preparation Time: 30 minutes

Serves: 2

Calories: 200 **Protein:** 3g **Sodium:** 40mg

Ingredients:

1 tablespoon olive oil

1 fennel bulb, chopped

2 carrots, chopped

1 onion, chopped

2 garlic cloves, minced

4 cups vegetable broth

Method of Preparation:

1. In a large pot, heat olive oil over medium heat.
2. Add fennel, carrots, onion, and garlic.

3. Cook until vegetables are softened.
4. Add vegetable broth and bring to a boil.
5. Reduce heat and simmer for 15-20 minutes, or until vegetables are tender.
6. Use an immersion blender to blend the soup until smooth.
7. Season with garlic.
8. Serve hot.

Chicken Gnocchi Soup

Preparation Time: 30 minutes

Serves: 2

Calories: 150 **Protein:** 15g **Sodium:** 60mg

Ingredients:

2 tablespoons butter

1/2 onion, chopped

2 carrots, chopped

2 celery stalks, chopped

2 garlic cloves, minced

4 cups chicken broth

1 cup cooked chicken breast, shredded

1 cup gnocchi

1/2 cup heavy cream

Method of Preparation:

1. In a large pot, melt butter over medium heat.
2. Add onion, carrots, celery, and garlic.
3. Cook until vegetables are softened.
4. Add chicken broth and bring to a boil.
5. Stir in cooked chicken breast and gnocchi.
6. Cook for 5-7 minutes, or until gnocchi is cooked through.
7. Cook for an additional 2-3 minutes, or soup is heated through.
8. Serve hot.

POULTRY MAINS

Garlic Peanut Butter Chicken with Parmesan Basmati Rice

Preparation Time: 45 minutes

Serves: 2

Calories: 40 **Protein:** 25g **Sodium:** 30mg

Ingredients:

2 chicken breasts

2 tablespoons peanut butter

2 cloves garlic, minced

1/4 cup soy sauce

1 tablespoon stevia

1 cup basmati rice

2 cups chicken broth

1/4 cup grated Parmesan cheese

Method of Preparation:

1. Preheat the oven to 375°F (190°C).
2. In a bowl, mix peanut butter, minced garlic, soy sauce, and stevia.
3. Coat chicken breasts with the peanut butter mixture and place in a baking dish.

4. In a separate pot, combine basmati rice and chicken broth. Bring to a boil, then reduce heat and simmer for 15-20 minutes, or until rice is cooked.
5. Stir in grated Parmesan cheese into the cooked rice.
6. Bake chicken breasts for 25-30 minutes, or until cooked through.
7. Serve chicken over Parmesan basmati rice.

One-Pan Chicken with Gravy

Preparation Time: 45 minutes

Serves: 2

Calories: 350 **Protein:** 20g **Sodium:** 400mg

Ingredients:

2 chicken thighs

1 onion, sliced

1 cup chicken broth

2 tablespoons flour

2 tablespoons butter

Method of Preparation:

1. In a skillet, melt butter over medium heat.
2. Add chicken thighs and onion slices.
3. Cook until chicken is browned.
4. Stir in flour until well combined.
5. Slowly pour in chicken broth, stirring constantly, until gravy thickens.
6. Cover and simmer for 20-25 minutes, or until chicken is cooked through.
7. Serve chicken with gravy.

Baked Chicken Drumsticks

Preparation Time: 40 minutes

Serves: 2

Calories: 300 **Protein:** 25g **Sodium:** 440mg

Ingredients:

4 chicken drumsticks

2 tablespoons olive oil

1 teaspoon garlic powder

1 teaspoon paprika

Method of Preparation:

1. Preheat the oven to 400°F (200°C).
2. In a bowl, mix olive oil, garlic powder, and paprika.
3. Coat chicken drumsticks with the olive oil mixture.
4. Place chicken drumsticks on a baking sheet lined with parchment paper.
5. Bake for 30-35 minutes, or until chicken is cooked through and juices run clear.
6. Serve hot.

Rosemary Turkey Bowl

Preparation Time: 45 minutes

Serves: 2

Calories: 350 **Protein:** 20g **Sodium:** 40mg

Ingredients:

2 turkey cutlets

1 tablespoon olive oil

2 cups cooked brown rice

1 cup steamed vegetables (e.g., broccoli, carrots)

1 teaspoon dried rosemary

Method of Preparation:

1. In a skillet, heat olive oil over medium heat.
2. Season turkey cutlets with dried rosemary.
3. Cook turkey cutlets for 5-6 minutes per side, or until cooked through.
4. In a bowl, layer cooked brown rice, steamed vegetables, and turkey cutlets.
5. Serve hot.

One-Pan Turkey and Potatoes

Preparation Time: 50 minutes

Serves: 2

Calories: 400 **Protein:** 25g **Sodium:** 40mg

Ingredients:

2 turkey breast slices

2 potatoes, peeled and diced

1 onion, sliced

1 tablespoon olive oil

1 teaspoon dried thyme

Method of Preparation:

1. Preheat the oven to 400°F (200°C).
2. In a large bowl, combine diced potatoes, sliced onion, olive oil, and dried thyme.
3. Spread the potato mixture evenly on a baking sheet lined with parchment paper.
4. Place turkey breast slices on top of the potato mixture.
5. Bake for 30-35 minutes, or until turkey is cooked through and potatoes are tender.
6. Serve hot.

SEAFOOD MAINS

Baked Salmon with Herbs

Preparation Time: 25 minutes

Serves: 2

Calories: 300 **Protein:** 25g **Sodium:** 40mg

Ingredients:

2 salmon fillets

2 tablespoons olive oil

1 teaspoon dried dill

1 teaspoon dried parsley

Method of Preparation:

1. Preheat the oven to 375°F (190°C).
2. In a small bowl, mix olive oil, dill, and parsley.
3. Place salmon fillets on a baking sheet lined with parchment paper.
4. Brush the salmon fillets with the olive oil mixture.
5. Bake for 15-20 minutes, or until salmon is cooked through and flakes easily with a fork.
6. Serve hot.

Grilled Shrimp Skewers

Preparation Time: 20 minutes

Serves: 2

Calories: 200 **Protein:** 20g **Sodium:** 30mg

Ingredients:

12 large shrimp, peeled and deveined

2 tablespoons olive oil

1 teaspoon paprika

Method of Preparation:

1. Preheat a grill or grill pan over medium-high heat.
2. In a bowl, mix olive oil, and paprika.
3. Thread shrimp onto skewers.
4. Brush shrimp with the olive oil mixture.
5. Grill shrimp skewers for 2-3 minutes per side, or until shrimp is pink and opaque.
6. Serve hot.

Poached Cod with Dill

Preparation Time: 20 minutes

Serves: 2

Calories: 250 **Protein:** 25g **Sodium:** 40mg

Ingredients:

2 cod fillets

2 cups fish or vegetable broth

1 tablespoon fresh dill

Method of Preparation:

1. In a large skillet, bring fish or vegetable broth to a simmer.
2. Add fresh dill to the broth.
3. Season cod fillets with herbs, then add them to the skillet.
4. Poach cod fillets for 8-10 minutes, or until fish is cooked through and flakes easily with a fork.
5. Serve hot.

Steamed Mussels in White Wine Sauce

Preparation Time: 15 minutes

Serves: 2

Calories: 300 **Protein:** 20g **Sodium:** 60mg

Ingredients:

2 pounds mussels, cleaned and debearded

1/2 cup white wine

2 cloves garlic, minced

2 tablespoons butter

1 tablespoon chopped fresh parsley

Method of Preparation:

1. In a large pot, bring white wine to a simmer.
2. Add garlic and butter to the pot.
3. Add mussels to the pot and cover with a lid.
4. Steam mussels for 5-7 minutes, or until they open.
5. Discard any unopened mussels.
6. Sprinkle chopped fresh parsley over the mussels.
7. Serve hot.

Broiled Flounder with Peanut Butter

Preparation Time: 15 minutes

Serves: 2

Calories: 250 **Protein:** 25g **Sodium:** 20mg

Ingredients:

2 flounder fillets

2 tablespoons melted butter

1 teaspoon dried parsley

Method of Preparation:

1. Preheat the broiler.
2. Place flounder fillets on a baking sheet lined with foil.
3. In a small bowl, mix melted butter, and dried parsley.
4. Brush the butter mixture over the flounder fillets.
5. Broil flounder fillets for 5-7 minutes, or until fish is cooked through and flakes easily with a fork.
6. Serve hot.

CONCLUSION

In conclusion, following an interstitial cystitis (IC) diet can be challenging but is essential for managing symptoms and improving quality of life.

The key is to identify and avoid trigger foods that can exacerbate symptoms, such as acidic, spicy, and high-caffeine foods.

Instead, focus on incorporating anti-inflammatory and soothing foods that can help alleviate discomfort.

Including plenty of fruits and vegetables, particularly those low in acidity like bananas, pears, and applesauce, can provide essential nutrients without irritating the bladder.

Whole grains, such as oats and brown rice, are also good choices for their fiber content and gentle effect on digestion.

When it comes to protein, lean options like chicken, turkey, and fish are preferable. Recipes like baked salmon with herbs or grilled shrimp skewers can be delicious and bladder-friendly choices.

Avoiding dairy products and opting for alternatives like almond or coconut milk can also help reduce bladder irritation.

Similarly, replacing salt with herbs and spices can add flavor without triggering symptoms.

Staying hydrated is crucial for bladder health, but it's important to choose beverages carefully. Water and herbal teas are excellent choices, while caffeinated and carbonated drinks should be avoided.

Printed in Great Britain
by Amazon